EUROPEAN COUNTRIES TODAY
ITALY

EUROPEAN COUNTRIES TODAY

TITLES IN THE SERIES

Austria	Italy
Belgium	Netherlands
Czech Republic	Poland
Denmark	Portugal
France	Spain
Germany	Sweden
Greece	United Kingdom
Ireland	European Union Facts & Figures

EUROPEAN COUNTRIES TODAY
ITALY

Dominic J. Ainsley

MASON CREST

Mason Crest
450 Parkway Drive, Suite D
Broomall, Pennsylvania PA 19008
(866) MCP-BOOK (toll free)

Copyright © 2019 by Mason Crest, an imprint of National Highlights, Inc. All rights reserved. No part of this publication may be reproduced or transmitted in any form or by any means, electronic or mechanical, including photocopying, recording, taping, or any information storage and retrieval system, without permission in writing from the publisher.

First printing
9 8 7 6 5 4 3 2 1

ISBN: 978-1-4222-3987-2
Series ISBN: 978-1-4222-3977-3
ebook ISBN: 978-1-4222-7802-4

Cataloging-in-Publication Data on file with the Library of Congress.

Printed in the United States of America

Cover images
Main: *Florence, Tuscany.*
Left: *Italian food products.*
Center: *The Tower of Pisa, Tuscany.*
Right: *Outdoor restaurant in Rome, Lazio.*

QR CODES AND LINKS TO THIRD-PARTY CONTENT

You may gain access to certain third-party content ("Third-Party Sites") by scanning and using the QR Codes that appear in this publication (the "QR Codes"). We do not operate or control in any respect any information, products, or services on such Third-Party Sites linked to by us via the QR Codes included in this publication, and we assume no responsibility for any materials you may access using the QR Codes. Your use of the QR Codes may be subject to terms, limitations, or restrictions set forth in the applicable terms of use or otherwise established by the owners of the Third-Party Sites. Our linking to such Third-Party Sites via the QR Codes does not imply an endorsement or sponsorship of such Third-Party Sites or the information, products, or services offered on or through the Third-Party Sites, nor does it imply an endorsement or sponsorship of this publication by the owners of such Third-Party Sites.

CONTENTS

Italy at a Glance	6
Chapter 1: Italy's Geography & Landscape	11
Chapter 2: The Government & History of Italy	23
Chapter 3: The Italian Economy	43
Chapter 4: Citizens of Italy: People, Customs & Culture	55
Chapter 5: The Famous Cities of Italy	69
Chapter 6: A Bright Future for Italy	81
Chronology	90
Further Reading & Internet Resources	91
Index	92
Picture Credits & Author	96

KEY ICONS TO LOOK FOR:

Words to Understand: These words with their easy-to-understand definitions will increase the reader's understanding of the text while building vocabulary skills.

Sidebars: This boxed material within the main text allows readers to build knowledge, gain insights, explore possibilities, and broaden their perspectives by weaving together additional information to provide realistic and holistic perspectives.

Educational Videos: Readers can view videos by scanning our QR codes, providing them with additional content to supplement the text. Examples include news coverage, moments in history, speeches, iconic sports moments, and much more!

Text-Dependent Questions: These questions send the reader back to the text for more careful attention to the evidence presented there.

Research Projects: Readers are pointed toward areas of further inquiry connected to each chapter. Suggestions are provided for projects that encourage deeper research and analysis.

ITALY AT A GLANCE

MAP OF EUROPE

The Geography of Italy

Location: southern Europe, a peninsula extending into the central Mediterranean Sea, northeast of Tunisia

Area: almost twice the size of Georgia; slightly larger than Arizona
  total: 116,347 square miles (301,340 sq. km);
land: 113,568 square miles (294,140 sq. km) including Sardinia and Sicily.
water: 2,779 square miles (7,200 sq. km)

Borders: Austria 156 miles (404 km), France 183 miles (476 km), Holy See (Vatican City) 1.3 miles (3.4 km), San Marino 14 miles (37 km), Slovenia 84 miles (218 km), Switzerland 269 miles (698 km)

Climate: predominantly Mediterranean; alpine in far north; hot, dry in south

Terrain: mostly rugged and mountainous; some plains, coastal lowlands

Elevation extremes:
  lowest point: lowest point: Mediterranean Sea 0 feet (0 m)
  highest point: Mont Blanc (Monte Bianco) de Courmayeur 15,577 feet (4,748 m)

Natural Hazards: regional risks including landslide, mudsfows, avalanches, earthquakes, volcanic eruptions, flooding

Source: www.cia.gov 2017

ITALY AT A GLANCE

Flag of Italy

Italy is dominated by two mountain ranges: the Alps and the Apennines, which are separated by fertile plains. The islands of Sardinia and Sicily being also part of Italy. The north and south of Italy are very different in terms of culture and wealth, the north being more prosperous than the south. Italy became a united country in 1861 when King Victor Emmanuel was proclaimed ruler. The flag dates back to Napoleonic times and was derived from the French tricolor, but with the blue stripe replaced by a green one, inspired by the shirts of the Milan militia. It has been said, however, that the green was chosen by Napoleon as a personal preference when he invaded Italy in the late eighteenth century.

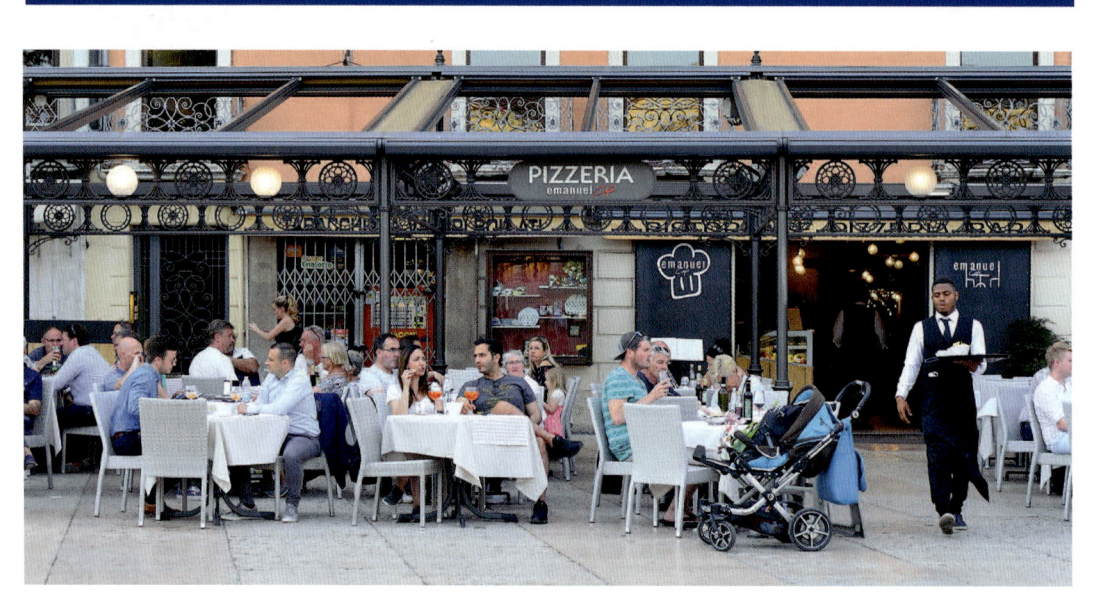

ABOVE: Italian towns and cities are famous for their outdoor cafés and restaurants. Italy's favorable climate means that diners can eat outside for many months of the year.

EUROPEAN COUNTRIES TODAY: ITALY

The People of Italy

Population: 62,137,802
Ethnic groups: Italian (includes small clusters of German-, French-, and Slovene-Italians in the north and Albanian-Italians and Greek-Italians in the south)
Age structure:
    0–14 years 13.65%
    15–64 years 64.82%
    65 years and above 21.53%
Population grown rate: 0.19%
Birth rate: 8.6 births/1,000 pop.
Death rate: 10.4 deaths/1,000 pop.
Migration rate: 3.7 migrants/1,000 pop.
Infant mortality rate: 3.3 deaths/1,000 live births
Life expectancy at birth:
    Total population: 79.4 years
    Male: 79.6 years
    Female: 85.1 years (2017 est.)
Total fertility rate: 1.44 children born/woman
Religions: Christian 80% (overwhelmingly Roman Catholic, with very small groups of Jehovah's Witnesses and Protestants), Muslim (about 800,000 to 1 million), atheist and agnostic 20%
Languages: Italian, German, French, Slovene
Literacy rate: 99.2%

Source: www.cia.gov 2017

Words to Understand

peninsula: A piece of land extending out into a body of water.

geographical: Of, or relating to geography.

avalanches: Large masses of snow, ice, etc., detached from mountain slopes that slide or fall suddenly downward.

BELOW: Tuscany is a region located in central Italy. It is famous for its beautiful landscapes, famous cities, medieval villages, and artistic heritage.

Chapter One
ITALY'S GEOGRAPHY & LANDSCAPE

The Italian **peninsula**, easily distinguishable on a map due to its well-known boot shape, encompasses 113,568 square miles (294,140 square kilometers) of land and 2,779 square miles (7,200 square kilometers) of water jutting out of Europe into the Mediterranean Sea. Italy's 1,141 miles (1,836 kilometers) of borders are shared by San Marino, Vatican City, France, Switzerland, Austria, and Slovenia. Italy's landscape is primarily rugged terrain, with less mountainous areas mostly near the coasts and around the large metropolitan areas. In fact, about three-quarters of Italy is mountainous or hilly, and the Italian Alps serve as a natural **geographical** barrier separating Italy from Slovenia, Austria, France, and Switzerland. The highest point in Italy is Monte Bianco de Courmayer, and the lowest point is the Mediterranean Sea. The Apennine Mountains run through the center of the country.

As a peninsula, Italy is surrounded on three sides by water. The Adriatic Sea to the east, the Ionian Sea to the south, and the Tyrrhenian and Ligurian seas to the west (each of these seas are part of the larger Mediterranean Sea) surround the

ABOVE: *The beautiful and sophisticated village Portofino, Liguria, is a holiday resort famous for its picturesque harbor and association with celebrities.*

11

ITALY'S GEOGRAPHY & LANDSCAPE

Educational Video

This video provides a brief insight into Italy's geography. Scan the QR code with your phone to watch!

ABOVE: *The beautiful village of Santa Maddalena is located in the Funes Valley, in the Dolomites mountain range.*

EUROPEAN COUNTRIES TODAY: ITALY

ABOVE: *Cagliari is the capital city of the Italian island of Sardinia. It's famous for the medieval hilltop citadel that overlooks the rest of the town.*

mainland of Italy; the Mediterranean Sea is on the east and south of the islands of Sardinia, Corsica, and Sicily. Italy has 1,500 lakes, the largest of which are Garda, Maggiore, and Como, all in the north. The longest river is the Po, which runs from the Alps to the Adriatic Sea. Another important river is the Tiber, which flows from the Apennine Mountains through the capital city of Rome before emptying into the Mediterranean Sea.

The Climate

Italy's climate attracts millions of tourists, who come to stay in the beautiful country throughout the year. The climate, due to its variations, provides something for almost everyone in search of different climatic destinations. The

ITALY'S GEOGRAPHY & LANDSCAPE

Mount Etna

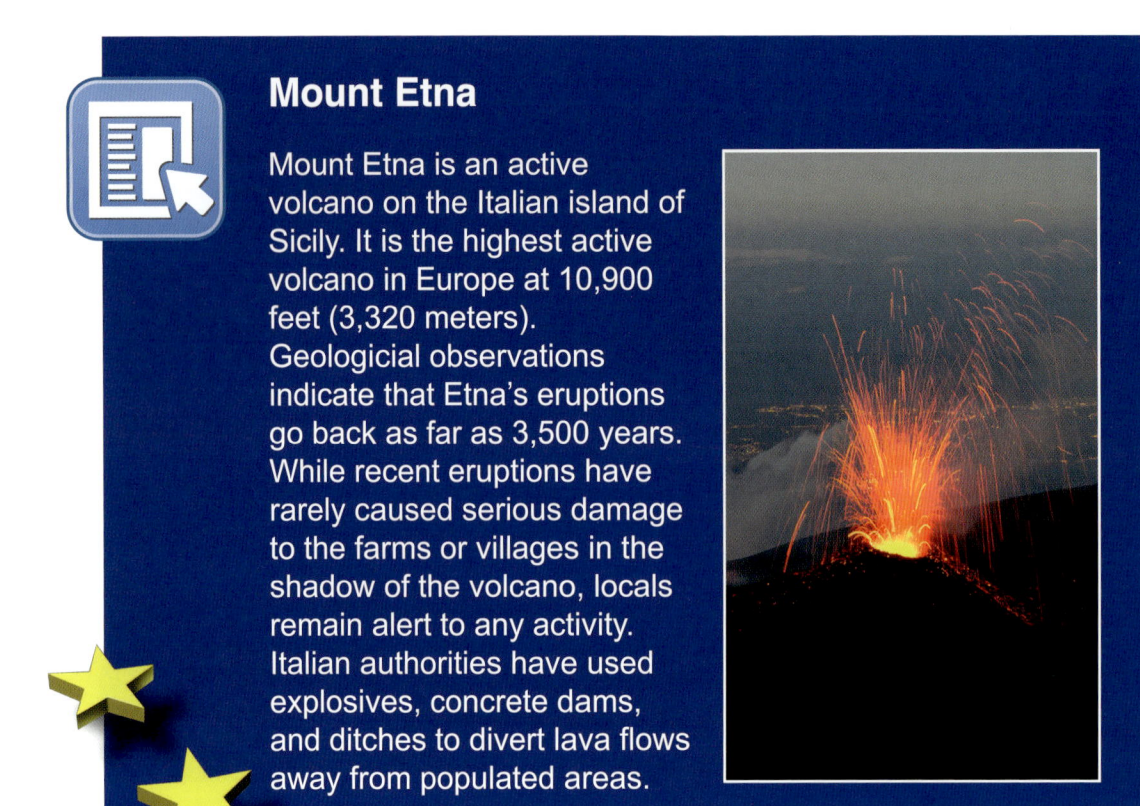

Mount Etna is an active volcano on the Italian island of Sicily. It is the highest active volcano in Europe at 10,900 feet (3,320 meters). Geologicial observations indicate that Etna's eruptions go back as far as 3,500 years. While recent eruptions have rarely caused serious damage to the farms or villages in the shadow of the volcano, locals remain alert to any activity. Italian authorities have used explosives, concrete dams, and ditches to divert lava flows away from populated areas.

northern parts of the country have an alpine climate, while the southern parts are hotter and drier. During the summer, northern Italy is warm and experiences plenty of rain, while the central portions of the country are quite humid, and southern Italy is hot and dry. During the winter, the north is cold and damp, with some areas reaching near-freezing temperatures, but the south has a mild winter, with temperatures rarely dipping below 50 degrees F (around 10 degrees C).

Natural Disasters

Natural disasters in Italy range from mudslides and **avalanches** to volcanic eruptions (Mount Vesuvius and Mount Etna are two well-known active volcanoes in Italy). The country has also suffered some catastrophic

14

EUROPEAN COUNTRIES TODAY: ITALY

ABOVE: *Pompeii in modern-day Campania was an ancient Roman city. It was destroyed in 79 CE when Mount Vesuvius erupted, burying the city under volcanic ash.*

ITALY'S GEOGRAPHY & LANDSCAPE

ABOVE: Many buildings were destroyed in the town of Norcia, in the region of Umbria, after a violent earthquake on October 30, 2016. The earthquake had a magnitude of 6.6. Its epicenter was close to the town.

earthquakes in recent years, for which it is prone. These environmental issues are largely due the mountainous terrain found in the nation. Sadly, pollution poses a significant threat to the countryside in which Italy takes pride.

Wildlife and Plants

Numerous forms of wildlife are present in Italy, but many have become endangered by overhunting. Foxes, wolves, black bears, and deer are present in many remote areas, and swallows, grouse, and falcons also live in these wild regions. In the seas, sardines, sharks, tuna, and anchovies are common. The

EUROPEAN COUNTRIES TODAY: ITALY

ABOVE: *The chamois is a goatlike species native to the mountains of Europe. It is commonly found in the Apennine Mountains.*

ITALY'S GEOGRAPHY & LANDSCAPE

Olive

Italy is famous for its ancient olive trees, some of them as old as two thousand years. The Romans were the first to plant olive trees in Italy and since those times, the olive has become a common sight throughout the Mediterranean. Homer (the Greek poet) describe olive oil as "liquid gold," referring to its properties in cooking, medicine, and skin care. Throughout the centuries, the olive tree has been given a special status and is considered a symbol of peace, abundance, and great natural power. Italy is a major producer of olive oil.

whale population is also making a comeback due to determined efforts by ecological societies. Increased awareness of environmental issues has prompted many Italians to reserve, preserve, and conserve. Many national parks have been established to create safe havens for animals that would otherwise have limited habitats.

    A team of scientists at Italy's University of Teramo successfully cloned a European mouflon, one of the smallest breeds of sheep in the world. The mouflon's native habitats are Corsica, Sardinia, and Cyprus, but the mouflon population in Europe is near extinction. Because of the success of the cloning,

EUROPEAN COUNTRIES TODAY: ITALY

ABOVE: *Piano Grande (Great Plain) mountain plateau in the Apennine Mountains, Umbria. The village of Castelluccio di Norcia is in the distance.*

ITALY'S GEOGRAPHY & LANDSCAPE

ABOVE: *A professional truffle hunter and his dog search for truffles in woodland in Tuscany. The truffle is a valuable type of edible fungus that is used in cooking.*

renewed efforts to determine the benefits of cloning endangered animals to preserve populations are under way.

Italy's best-known floral icon is the olive tree, with 15 million of these trees growing across the country's landscape. The Romans spread olive trees across the entire peninsula, and the oldest olive trees in Italy are over 2,000 years old. Recently, many have been stolen by tree thieves who sell them on the black market to wealthy European collectors. Because of the sheer number of olive trees, the Italian government is finding it difficult to act against the removal of what some consider to be part of Italy's heritage. Olive trees aren't the only things that have fallen prey to the black market: mushrooms, truffles, and bounty from Italy's botanical gardens are also quite popular in the underground market.

Text-Dependent Questions

1. Which seas surround Italy?

2. What is the longest river in Italy?

3. How long can an olive tree live for?

Research Project

Write a report about the eruption of Mount Vesuvius and the city of Pompeii.

Words to Understand

Neolithic: Relating to the latest period of the Stone Age, characterized by polished stone implements.

satiate: To satisfy a need fully or to excess.

suffrage: The right to vote in an election.

BELOW: The Roman Forum, dating from the sixth century BCE, was ancient Rome's grand political center and a district of temples and basilicas. The Roman Forum is one of the most renowned archaeological sites in the world and it is fascinating to learn that it is where the Roman Empire began.

Chapter Two
THE GOVERNMENT & HISTORY OF ITALY

Italy has a rich history that stretches back to prehistoric times. During the **Neolithic** period, small agricultural-based communities replaced the hunter-gatherers of the Paleolithic and Mesolithic periods. Settlers from the east introduced the use of metal to the peninsula during the Bronze Age. With the arrival of these newcomers came distinct regional identities, which developed by 1000 BCE when the use of iron became prevalent.

Indo-European-speaking tribes began to arrive in what is now known as Italy late in the Neolithic period. These tribes, such as those speaking Latin and Venetic, settled in the peninsula but would be forced to wait their turn to exert any extensive influence over their neighbors. The indigenous non-Indo-European Etruscans extended a wide influence over the central portion of the peninsula and even dominated and ruled many Latin communities. Later Roman historians note that the Etruscans ruled the city of Rome for a many years, and it

ABOVE: *This statue of Neptune, Roman god of the sea, is part of the Trevi Fountain, Rome.*

THE GOVERNMENT & HISTORY OF ITALY

Julius Caesar was the greatest ruler of the Roman republic. A brilliant general and politician, he extended and solidified Roman rule into the Iberian Peninsula, Britannia, and the main portions of the remainder of Europe. During these events, Rome was still a republic ruled by the Senate, many of whom believed Caesar was growing too powerful. In 44 BCE, a group of senators murdered the popular Caesar, and after a period of civil unrest, his nephew and adopted son Octavius marched on Rome and forced the Senate to name him consul. He would eventually become the first Roman emperor, after first sharing leadership with Julius Caesar's general, Marc Antony, and Marcus Lepidus. Under Octavius, who was renamed "Augustus," the Roman Empire expanded to rule most of the known world. This empire would last for hundreds of years, until internal strife and external threats from Germanic tribes weakened the once-great empire.

The Fall of Rome

Because of political corruption, selfish emperors, and other undermining internal factors, Rome's power began to decline. The generals of the formerly invincible army cared more for their

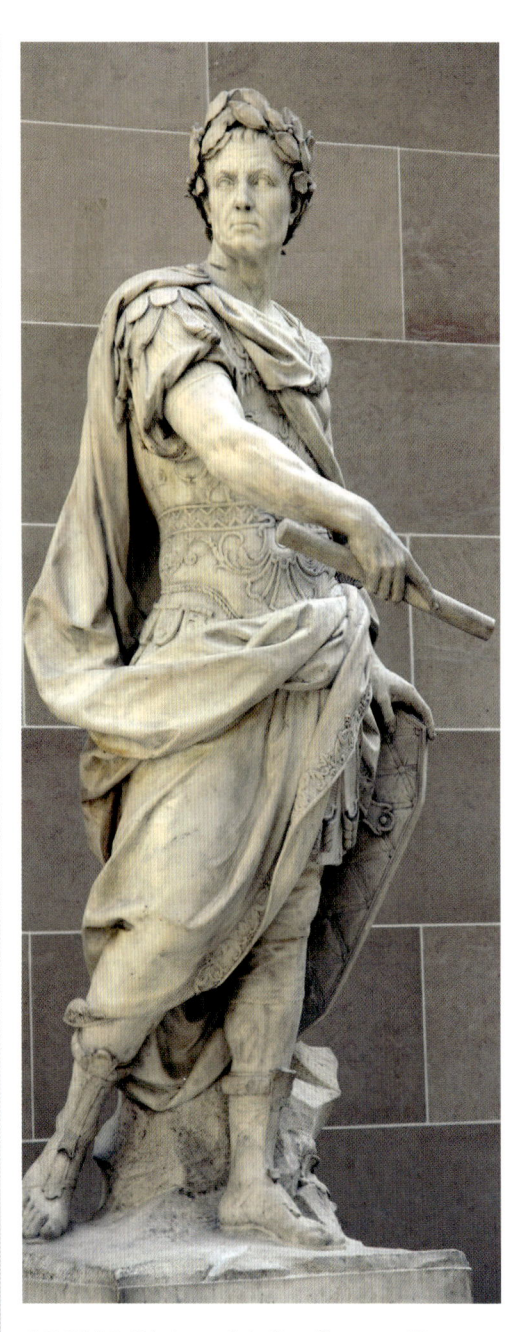

ABOVE: *Statue of Julius Caesar, Roman general and statesman. The Louvre, Paris.*

EUROPEAN COUNTRIES TODAY: ITALY

ABOVE: The Death of Julius Caesar *by Vincenzo Camuccini. Caesar was assassinated on the Ides of March (March 15) 44 BCE.*

villas and estates than their legions' well-being and success. Weakened armies meant the barbaric Germanic tribes no longer needed to live in fear of repercussions of rebellion. They began to revolt, and without competent generals abroad or a stable emperor at home (from 186 CE to 286 CE, thirty-seven different emperors ruled, and twenty-five of those were assassinated), the empire plunged into disarray. The movement of gold into the coffers of Rome slowed as Rome stopped conquering new lands, but wealthy Romans continued to spend gold on luxury items. Because of this outflow of precious metal, less gold was available for use in minting coins, and the value of minted money dropped. This caused inflation, as merchants raised the prices of their goods. All these causes, and more—such as the spliting of the empire into the Roman and Byzantine empires—led to the sacking of Rome in 476 CE, during the reign of Romulus Augustus. The Roman Empire was no more.

The Tower of Pisa

One of Italy's most recognizable sights is the Tower of Pisa. The bell tower of the city's cathedral, it sits in Pisa's *Campo dei Miracoli*, Field of Miracles.
Work began on the tower in 1173 and continued for almost two hundred years, with a couple of long interruptions.

For many years, it was believed that the leaning was a "design element," but it is now known that the tower was meant to stand erect. The leaning began while it was being built, and many construction mechanisms were tried to prevent the tilt. Nothing worked. Efforts are still underway to stop the inclination from progressing. Today's efforts are focused on the subsoil beneath and around the tower.

Even if the tower were straight, it would still be one of the most impressive sights in the country. But there wouldn't be the traditional photographs of tourists holding up the tower to keep it from falling.

THE GOVERNMENT & HISTORY OF ITALY

ABOVE: *This portrait is likely to be of Christopher Columbus and is the only portrait of the explorer. By Sebastiano del Piombo.*

Medieval Italy

After the fall of Rome, the Byzantine Empire in the east continued the legacies of both Rome and Greece, but control of Italy was eventually lost to the invading Lombards. Italy once again splintered into ethnic strongholds. The Lombards, a Germanic tribe, ruled an extensive portion of the peninsula until the papacy invited the Franks (another Germanic tribe) to invade Italy in order to restore land that the Church had lost. This began the rule of the Holy Roman Empire (under Charlemagne) in Europe. Around this time, Arabs from North Africa conquered Sicily, but they were eventually expelled by the Normans, who established a kingdom on the small island.

Strong city-states began to arise in Italy during the Middle Ages. Florence, Milan, and Venice, among others, grew powerful through trade, and Italy was effectively splintered into regional rule. Strong and wealthy families in the city-states began to rule and gain influence. In 1494, two years after Italian Cristoforo Colombo (Christopher Columbus) discovered the New World, Charles VIII of France invaded Italy, ending the wars between rival city-states and beginning a long period of foreign rule. The Habsburg Dynasty brought most of Italy under control, and when the dynasty was divided between Emperor Ferdinand I and King Philip II of Spain, Philip inherited Italy. In the early 1700s, Austria annexed Italy in the War of the Spanish Succession (1701–14). Small parts of Italy began gaining independence from foreign rule, but the nation remained fragmented with separately ruled regions.

EUROPEAN COUNTRIES TODAY: ITALY

Unification of Italy

Foreign rule made the dwellers of the Italian Peninsula desire freedom. Revolutions by the Carbonari, a radical group, were quelled by the Austrians, as were the revolutions of 1848, in which the king of Sardinia declared Italy free and created a constitution. In 1859, with the backing of France and England (who saw an Austrian defeat as favorable to their political interests), Sardinia led the battle for Italian independence against Austria with the help of Giuseppe Garibaldi, who led his "Redshirts" to the southern part of the peninsula and captured it. Then, showing his true patriotism, Garibaldi handed it over to King Emmanuel II of Sardinia. The Kingdom of Italy was formed officially in 1861.

The new nation had many internal problems. Its citizens thought of themselves not as Italians, but as part of the region of their birth and ancestry. The country was in debt, and the pope refused to recognize the new nation, furious over the seizure of papal lands. The northern portion of the country developed to a greater extent than the southern portion. Crime and social activism increased as the poorer south seemed stuck in its misery. The people were for the most part poor and illiterate, and the nation had nothing in terms of international prestige or recognition. In an attempt to gain status as a colonial power, Italy foolishly attacked the stronger African nation of Ethiopia and was embarrassed on an international level as they were defeated soundly in the 1890s. Italy apparently failed to learn its lesson as it went on to declare war on Turkey over the North African nation

ABOVE: *Giuseppe Garibaldi was a general, politician, and nationalist who played an important role in the history of Italy.*

THE GOVERNMENT & HISTORY OF ITALY

ABOVE: Benito Mussolini, with a group of fascist leaders, led the March on Rome in October 1922. From left to right: Michele Bianchi, Emilio De Bono, Benito Mussolini, Italo Balbo, and Cesare Maria De Vecchi.

of Libya in 1911. During World War I, Italy joined the Allies only to suffer staggering losses of men and machines during the course of the war. The postwar failure of the Allies to provide lands that Italy had been promised on joining the Allied war effort led to a generally disgruntled Italian population, laying down the foundations for Benito Mussolini and fascism to take control of the nation.

The Rise of Fascism

Benito Mussolini began the fascist movement in Italy. His "Blackshirts," a squad of thugs who terrorized those whose views differed from Mussolini, helped him gain strength in the troubled nation. King Victor Emmanuel III named Mussolini prime minister in 1922, and within several years the nation had been transformed into a military state by the new regime. In 1935, Mussolini sent troops back to Ethiopia to compensate for the embarrassing military fiasco of the 1890s, and the following year Italian troops were sent to Spain to aid Francisco Franco in the Spanish Civil War. German dictator Adolf Hitler formed the Rome-Berlin Pact in 1936, and both dictators continued to **satiate** their aggressive land-seizing propensities as Hitler annexed Alsace-Lorraine and the Sudetenland, while Mussolini added Albania to Italy's territory. The English prime minister, Neville Chamberlain, and his French allies continued to appease the two obvious threats, and the result of this was the outbreak of World War II when Hitler attacked Poland, with Mussolini joining the war on the German side several months later.

World War II

During World War II, Italy's meager conquests were generally overshadowed by the stronger successes of the German *blitzkrieg*, or lightning war. The overall incompetence of Italy's army was an embarrassing contrast to Rome's past military prowess. The Allies invaded Italy in 1943, and Mussolini was expelled to a puppet government in the northern part of the nation after King Victor Emmanuel III forced him to resign. Mussolini was captured and executed by Communist partisans during the final stages of the Allied expulsion of the German army from Italy.

Postwar Italy

The monarchy was abolished in 1946 and a new republican constitution was drafted. The United States gave a great deal of aid to Italy as a part of the Marshall Plan, and, because of this, the Italian economy grew considerably. Industrial expansion and economic growth resulted in a higher standard of living for the average Italian citizen. However, the 1970s saw a return to labor unrest and political agitation. Extremist groups seemed to be on the rise until the mid- to late 1980s under the premiership of Bettino Craxi, when the economy made a recovery.

THE GOVERNMENT & HISTORY OF ITALY

ABOVE: The Palazzo Montecitorio, Rome, is the seat of the Chamber of Deputies. The debating chamber has been decorated with decorative glass in the art nouveau style.

EUROPEAN COUNTRIES TODAY: ITALY

The Italian Government

Today, the Italian form of government is a republic. Universal **suffrage** has been granted to all citizens over the age of eighteen, but for senatorial elections the minimum age requirement is twenty-five years of age. The executive branch of the government consists of the president, the Council of Ministers, and the prime minister, who is also the president of the Council of Ministers. The Italian parliament and fifty-eight regional representatives form an electoral college, which elects the president for a seven-year term. The president in turn nominates a prime minister, who must be approved by parliament. He also nominates a Council of Ministers to be approved by the president.

The *parlamento*, or parliament, is comprised of the *Senato della Repubblica*, or Senate, and the *Camera dei Deputati*, or Chamber of Deputies, in a bicameral configuration. There are a number of senators for life, a classification all former presidents are placed in. The senators serve five-year terms, as do legislators in the Chamber of Deputies.

The judicial branch of the government is composed of the *Corte Costituzionale*, or Constitutional Court. This court has five judges appointed by the president, five elected by the parliament, and five elected from supreme courts.

President Sergio Mattarella was elected on February 3, 2015, and Prime Minister Paolo Gentiloni was elected on December 12, 2016. There are myriad political parties in the government with many parties forming coalitions with other parties, creating party conglomerates such as the Daisy Alliance, which was formed by the Italian Popular Party, the Italian Renewal Party, the Union of Democrats for Europe, and the Democrats.

Italy and the European Union (EU)

Italy is a founding member of the EU, and has held the presidency of the EU many times. As an original member, Italy holds an important position in the EU and has been a strong supporter of it. However, it does not always agree with other European nations as to how the EU's government should function.

One of the big issues in the EU is similar to one that the United States faces as well: who should have more power, the central government (the EU in

THE GOVERNMENT & HISTORY OF ITALY

Europe, or Washington, D.C., in the United States) or the individual members (the nations of Europe or the states of the United States)?

When all the EU members' governments have to agree before any member can take action, that's known as intergovernmentalism; everyone works together to form the central government's laws and policies. In the EU, the opposite approach is called supranationalism, which is where the member countries make their own decisions regarding many laws and policies; in other words, the individual countries have more power than the central government does. The EU uses both these methods, but some EU nations generally support one approach over the other. Italy has supported a supranational approach, along with several other European nations, notably France. Other EU nations want the central government to be able to make more decisions that would apply to the entire EU.

The conflict between these two approaches often becomes more obvious when smaller issues arise. In the United States, it came to a head in the 1800s over the issue of slavery, causing the Civil War, but it continues to be an

The Italian Government

On January 1, 1948, Italy adopted a constitutional charter, which defines the political and civil liberties of citizens and the principles of government. The Italian parliament is divided into three houses: the seat of government where the president resides in the Palazzo del Quirinale, the chamber of deputies at the Palazzo Montecitorio, and the senate at the Palazzo Madama. Italy is headed by a president, a public figure with little power. The president appoints a prime minister, the elected head of government. The current prime minster is Paolo Gentiloni, who has been in office since December 12, 2016.

EUROPEAN COUNTRIES TODAY: ITALY

ABOVE: *The Italian prime minister, Paolo Gentiloni, photographed in 2017.*

THE GOVERNMENT & HISTORY OF ITALY

important question whenever states don't agree on a particular issue, such as same-sex marriage or abortion rights. The smaller issues in Europe are different (they often have to do with the rights of ethnic minorities, with the environment, and with money), but the big issue is very much the same. Will the EU be able to consolidate its power the way the United States did—or will it continue to act as many separate nations? That question still hasn't been settled.

Modern Politics in Italy

Italy's current prime minister is Paolo Gentiloni who has been in office since December 12, 2016. He is a member of the Democratic party. He served as minster for foreign affairs from October 2014 until when he became prime minster. One of the most important challenges for Gentiloni to contend with is

ABOVE: *The Palazzo del Quirinale in Rome is the official residence of the president.*

EUROPEAN COUNTRIES TODAY: ITALY

the high level of immigration to Italy from Libya. He has also has other problems including a banking crisis at home, the European debt crisis, and the insurgency of the so-called Islamic State in the Middle East.

Unfortunately, Italy has always had problems acting as a unified whole, which makes it difficult for real change to come to this beautiful and historic nation. Most Italians identify far more with their family, town, or local region than they do with their nation as a whole—and few Italians identify with the EU at all. This has made Italy's politics fragmented and ineffective; since World War II, the country has had more than sixty different governments, each one rising and falling, with little continuity between them. With so many starts and stops, it's hard for the nation to make progress!

Because of this, Italy faces many dilemmas. Its economy is one of its biggest problems—and yet, despite that, Italians enjoy one of the world's highest standards of living. Italy's fashion, luxury cars and motorcycles, furniture, tourism, design, and food still help set the entire world's standards.

Text-Dependent Questions

1. Why was Julius Caesar murdered?

2. Who executed Benito Mussolini?

3. What nationality was Christopher Columbus?

Research Project

Using the Internet and textbooks as sources, write a biography of Julius Caesar.

THE GOVERNMENT & HISTORY OF ITALY

The Formation of the European Union (EU)

The EU is a confederation of European nations that continues to grow. As of 2017, there are twenty-eight official members. Several other candidates are also waiting for approval. All countries that enter the EU agree to follow common laws about foreign security policies. They also agree to cooperate on legal matters that go on within the EU. The European Council meets to discuss all international matters and make decisions about them. Each country's own concerns and interests are important, though. And apart from legal and financial issues, the EU tries to uphold values such as peace, human dignity, freedom, and equality.

All member countries remain autonomous. This means that they generally keep their own laws and regulations. The idea for a union among European nations was first mentioned after World War II. The war had devastated much of Europe, both physically and financially. In 1950, the French foreign minister suggested that France and West Germany combine their coal and steel industries under one authority. Both countries would have control over the

ABOVE: *The entrance to the European Union Parliament Building in Brussels.*

EUROPEAN COUNTRIES TODAY: ITALY

Member Countries

Austria	Greece	Romania
Belgium	Hungary	Slovakia
Bulgaria	Ireland	Slovenia
Croatia	Italy	Spain
Cyprus	Latvia	Sweden
Czech Republic	Lithuania	United Kingdom
Denmark	Luxembourg	*(Brexit: For the time*
Estonia	Malta	*being, the United*
Finland	Netherlands	*Kingdom remains a full*
France	Poland	*member of the EU.)*
Germany	Portugal	

industries. This would help them become more financially stable. It would also make war between the countries much more difficult. The idea was interesting to other European countries as well. In 1951, France, West Germany, Belgium, Luxembourg, the Netherlands, and Italy signed the Treaty of Paris, creating the European Coal and Steel Community. These six countries would become the core of the EU.

In 1957, these same countries signed the Treaties of Rome, creating the European Economic Community. In 1965, the Merger Treaty formed the European Community. Finally, in 1992, the Maastricht Treaty was signed. This treaty defined the European Union. It gave a framework for expanding the EU's political role, particularly in the area of foreign and security policy. It would also replace national currencies with the euro. The next year, the treaty went into effect. At that time, the member countries included the original six plus another six who had joined during the 1970s and '80s.

In the following years, the EU would take more steps to form a single market for its members. This would make joining the union even more advantageous. In addition to enlargement, the EU is steadily becoming more integrated through its own policies for closer cooperation between member states.

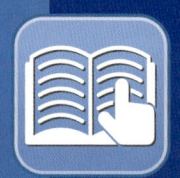

Words to Understand

service sector: The sector of the economy that provides services rather than products.

viability: Capable of becoming actual or useful.

unification: The act, process, or result of bringing or coming together.

BELOW: The province of Asti is in the Piedmont region of northern Italy. Asti is an important wine-making area producing both red and white wines. It produces the famous sparkling Asti wines, including the Moscato d'Asti and the Spumante.

Chapter Three
THE ITALIAN ECONOMY

Since the **unification** of Italy in 1861, the northern regions of the country have always enjoyed greater prosperity and industrial **viability** than the southern regions. The southern, more agricultural regions lack the industry and private companies that the north has always possessed. Italy's natural resources include coal, zinc, and marble, and the surrounding presence of water has allowed the fishing industry to grow.

ABOVE: The world-famous Carrara marble is mined in Carrara, Tuscany. Marble has been mined in this area since ancient times. The sculptor Michelangelo used Carrara marble for some of his works.

THE ITALIAN ECONOMY

In 2016, Italy's gross domestic product (GDP) was US$1,851 trillion. The 2016 per capita GDP, the country's total GDP divided into the total population, was US$36,800. The main sources of Italy's GDP are 73.8 percent from the service sector, 24.1 percent from industry, and 2.1 percent from agriculture.

The employment of Italy's labor force of 25.8 million reflects the importance of the **service sector** and industrial sector to Italy's economy. Approximately 67.8 percent of the workforce is employed in the service sector, and about 28.3 percent work in industry. Only about 3.9 percent of the workforce is employed in agriculture-related occupations.

ABOVE: *Maranello is a town in the region of Emilia-Romagna in northern Italy. The town is best known as the base for Scuderia Ferrari, the official name for Ferrari's racing division.*

EUROPEAN COUNTRIES TODAY: ITALY

Tourism

More than 50 million people vist Italy per year. In fact, it is the fifth most visited country in the world. People visit Italy for its rich culture, cuisine, history, fashion, and art. It it also famous for its beautiful coastlines, mountains, and beautiful countryside. Italy is home to fifty-three World Heritage Sites, and cities such as Venice and Florence are in the world's top one hundred destinations to visit.

Italy's major industries include tourism, chemical production, textiles and design of fine apparel, and motor vehicle production. The predominant agricultural products generated in Italy are beef, dairy products, fruits and vegetables, and fish.

Some of Italy's main trading partners are Germany, France, Spain, and the United States. Among Italy's lucrative exports are luxury cars; Italy is a world leader in their production. Car brands such as Ferrari, Alfa Romeo, Maserati, and Fiat are exported to almost every country in the world. These cars have given Italy a reputation for luxury products over the years; many of these car companies date back to the early 1900s.

Most of Italy's energy needs must be met by imports; Italy produces only 70,670 barrels per day (bbl/day) of oil, while importing 1.2 million bbl/day. The nation also produces 5.7 billion cubic meters of natural gas and consumes 70.9 billion cubic meters of natural gas. Much of the oil and gas required for Italy is imported. Italy has 769 miles (1,241 kilometers) of crude oil pipeline and 11,373 miles (18,343 kilometers) of natural gas pipeline.

Since the construction of its first railroad in 1839, Italy has developed its rail system into one of the most impressive in Europe. Most rail stations in Italy are

THE ITALIAN ECONOMY

ABOVE: *Milan Central railroad station was designed by Ulisse Stacchini. The station was completed in 1931. It was inspired by the baths at Caracalla in Rome and influenced by some of the magificent railroad stations in the United States.*

famous for their beautiful architecture. Italy has international rail links to France, Austria, Switzerland, and Slovenia. There have also been discussions for possibly building an underwater subway system from Sicily to Tunisia.

With 302,374 miles (487,700 kilometers) of roadways, over-the-road transport of goods is easily accomplished. Italy has many harbors and ports along its coastline, and has 132 airports, making ship and air transport viable options as well.

Italy's Economy and the Global Recession

In 2008, the United States economy entered a slowdown period. Many companies made less money or went out of business altogether. As a result, there were fewer jobs, and unemployment soared. Because many people were out of work, they had less money to spend, which meant that businesses did

EUROPEAN COUNTRIES TODAY: ITALY

ABOVE: Every year, Italy's stunning cities (such as Venice) are flooded with visitors, which is vital to Italy's economy.

THE ITALIAN ECONOMY

even worse, creating a vicious circle that led to what economists call a recession. And because the economies of the world are so linked together, with nations trading with each other and many businesses operating in countries all around the world, the recession soon spread from the United States around the globe. As a result, the EU's economy also entered a recession. Italy was one of the European nations that was in the biggest trouble.

Other EU countries—like Greece, Portugal, and Ireland—might have had worse problems, but Italy's economy was more important to both the EU and

ABOVE: *The central business district of Milan. The UniCredit building is in the distance.*

EUROPEAN COUNTRIES TODAY: ITALY

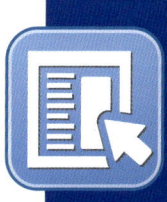

The Economy of Italy

Gross Domestic Product (GDP): $$2.23 trillion (2016 est.)
GDP Per Capita: $36,800 (2016 est.)
Industries: tourism, machinery, iron and steel, chemicals, food processing, textiles, motor vehicles, clothing, footwear, ceramics
Agriculture: fruits, vegetables, grapes, potatoes, sugar beet, soybeans, grain, olives; beef, dairy products; fish
Export Commodities: engineering products, textiles and clothing, production machinery, motor vehicles, transport equipment, chemicals; foodstuffs, beverages, and tobacco; minerals, nonferrous metals
Export Partners: Germany 12.6%, France 10.5%, US 8.9%, UK 5.4%, Spain 5%, Switzerland 4.6% (2016)
Import Commodities: engineering products, chemicals, transport equipment, energy products, minerals and nonferrous metals, textiles and clothing; food, beverages, tobacco
Import Partners: Germany 16.3%, France 8.9%, China 7.5%, Netherlands 5.5%, Spain 5.3%, Belgium 4.9% (2016)
Currency: euro

Source: www.cia.gov 2017

the entire world, so, in a way, its economic problems were more frightening. The Italian economy is the seventh largest in the world, which means that when Italy has problems, those problems affect many other nations as well. During the EU's recession, UniCredit, a European banking group, said that Italy was "the swing factor" that would determine how well the EU emerged from the recession. Italy, said UniCredit, was "the largest of the vulnerable countries, and most vulnerable of the large" nations in the EU. By 2010, most of the EU

THE ITALIAN ECONOMY

was coming out of the recession, but economists were still keeping a worried eye on Italy.

Many experts point to Italy's culture as being partly responsible for its economic problems. Just as Italy has had trouble uniting socially and politically, it also has trouble working together toward common economic goals. Italians are loyal to their individual communities, and even more loyal to their own

Did You Know?

Did you know you can't get Parmesan cheese or Chianti wine just anywhere. There are international laws to prevent attaching names such as Parmesan or Chianti to cheese and wine produced outside the region. To be truly Parmesan cheese, it must be produced in the Parma region of Italy. Chianti wine is produced from grapes grown in the Chianti region of Tuscany.

EUROPEAN COUNTRIES TODAY: ITALY

ABOVE: Many Italian businesses are family-run and often relatively small. This grocery stall is in Ballarò market in Palermo, Sicily.

families. They protect what they see as their family's, even at the cost of hurting their nation as a whole. Many businesses are controlled by family-run guilds that keep outsiders out of the jobs. Italian businesspeople tend to care very little about growth; they hate risk; and they want to keep things exactly the way they've always been. As a result, people who do not belong to a rich, powerful family often have few opportunities, and many of the best and brightest young people are leaving Italy altogether.

All this makes for an outdated and shaky economy that may not be able to survive the challenges of the twenty-first century. And yet Italy has a rich culture that could help make it strong.

Words to Understand

frescoes: Paintings created by painting on wet plaster.

gastronomic: Relating to food and cookery, especially the art of good eating.

opulent: Having or indicating wealth.

BELOW: Florence is considered to be the birthplace of the Renaissance. Politically, economically, and culturally, it was the most important city in Europe for over two centuries. The famous Ponte Vecchio (Old Bridge) is in the foreground.

Chapter Four
CITIZENS OF ITALY: PEOPLE, CUSTOMS & CULTURE

Many different ethnicities and cultures are represented among the 62 million inhabitants of Italy. This is in part due to the almost perpetual foreign rule that the nation has been under for much of its history. Recent immigration has added to the country's rich diversity. The majority of people are Italian, but there are clusters of German-Italians, Greek-Italians, French-Italians, and Slovene-Italians. Most ethnic groups are bilingual, speaking Italian along with their native languages. (The Greek-Italians in the southern regions and Sicily are descendants of the Greeks who in ancient times migrated to and colonized the

ABOVE: *In Italy, social life is centered around the family. The importance of food, drink, and meal times makes Italian culture distinctive.*

CITIZENS OF ITALY: PEOPLE, CUSTOMS & CULTURE

ABOVE: Marriage it an important tradition in Italy and, as Italy is such a beautiful country, many overseas couples choose it as a destination for their wedding day.

portions of Italy that became known as Magna Grecia; they speak Griko, a language descended from Greek.) The island of Sicily's inhabitants are ethnically a mix of Italians, Greeks, Phoenicians, and Arabs; some also have Norman, Spanish, and Albanian ancestry. Sicilian is a distinct Romance language spoken by most of its inhabitants, although it is spoken less and less as a first language, since the Italian spoken in public schools takes precedence among the youth.

A large influx of recent, mostly illegal immigrants from the continent of Africa is increasing the ethnic diversity of Italy. Although many new residents are from North Africa, an increasing number are of sub-Saharan origin living primarily in large cities such as Rome. The North African immigration is increasing Italy's Muslim population.

EUROPEAN COUNTRIES TODAY: ITALY

Educational Video

Twelve fun facts about Italian history, traditions, and cuisine.

ABOVE: *The Venice Carnival takes place annually. It ends with the Christian celebration of Lent on Shrove Tuesday, forty days before Easter. The festival is world famous for its elaborate masks and beautiful costumes.*

CITIZENS OF ITALY: PEOPLE, CUSTOMS & CULTURE

The persecution of Kurds in Turkey in recent years has caused an increase in Kurdish migration to Italy. Italy has been criticized by other EU member states such as Germany on its seemingly open-door policy toward unauthorized Kurdish immigration. These EU member states claim that illegal Kurdish immigration to Italy, when coupled with the open borders among all EU nations, results in a wave of illegal Kurdish immigration to other EU nations—immigration the other nations may not be able to accommodate.

Most of Italy's population is Roman Catholic. However, the Protestant, Jewish, and Muslim communities are small but growing.

Art, Architecture, Literature, and Music

Italy has a rich history of art, architecture, and literature. In the fourteenth century, the Renaissance began in Italy. Beginning in the city of Florence in northern Italy, the Renaissance spread to the remainder of Italy and then to the rest of Europe, effectively ending the Dark Ages. The Renaissance, which means "rebirth" in French, was a period in which new ways of thinking and new artistic and literary methods of expressing those new thoughts were developed. Italy holds an illustrious place among those countries that

ABOVE: *Niccolò Machiavelli by Santi di Tito.*

ABOVE: *Leonardo da Vinci, self-portrait.*

EUROPEAN COUNTRIES TODAY: ITALY

produced well-known Renaissance thinkers. Works from influential thinkers such as Machiavelli, author of *The Art of War* and *The Prince*, and art from the likes of Michelangelo, who created the famous nude statue of the Hebrew King David and the ceiling **frescoes** of Rome's Sistine Chapel, are renowned worldwide. The futuristic designs of Leonardo da Vinci, whose notebooks even contain plans for a rudimentary helicopter, and his world-famous artworks, including *Mona Lisa* and *The Last Supper,* were also among the products of the Italian Renaissance.

Italy is widely known as the birthplace of opera. Traditionally, most opera is performed in Italian. Opera was exported to other nations in Europe, and the result is many non-Italian composers have written operas. However, Italians such as Giuseppe Verdi and Giacomo Puccini remain favorites of opera lovers worldwide.

Another Italian contribution to music is the invention of the pianoforte, or piano, sometime in the late 1600s by Bartolomeo Cristoforo of Florence. The piano would soon develop into the primary instrument of composers in the latter part of the baroque period, and lasting through the classical period. Some of the most beautiful pieces in the European musical repertoire are written for piano.

The Italian influence extends to music notation. All performance instructions are written in Italian. For example, the notation instructing the individual playing the music to play loudly is *forte*, the Italian word for loud.

ABOVE: Mona Lisa (La Gioconda) *by Leonardo da Vinci.*

CITIZENS OF ITALY: PEOPLE, CUSTOMS & CULTURE

Today's Italian youth listen to a variety of musical genres. Italian rap and hip-hop are enjoying a considerable growth in popularity as Italian artists decide to venture into these wildly popular American genres for themselves. Rock and roll is another import of American origin, with Italian stars such as Zucchero enjoying immense popularity not only in Italy but in the rest of Europe also. Traditional folk artists are also popular among all ages in Italy, and Patchanka, an Italian mix of punk, reggae, and rock, often with politically charged lyrics, is another frequently heard musical genre.

ABOVE: *Teatro alla Scala (La Scala) is a famous opera house in Milan where the works of Puccini and Verdi are regularly performed.*

EUROPEAN COUNTRIES TODAY: ITALY

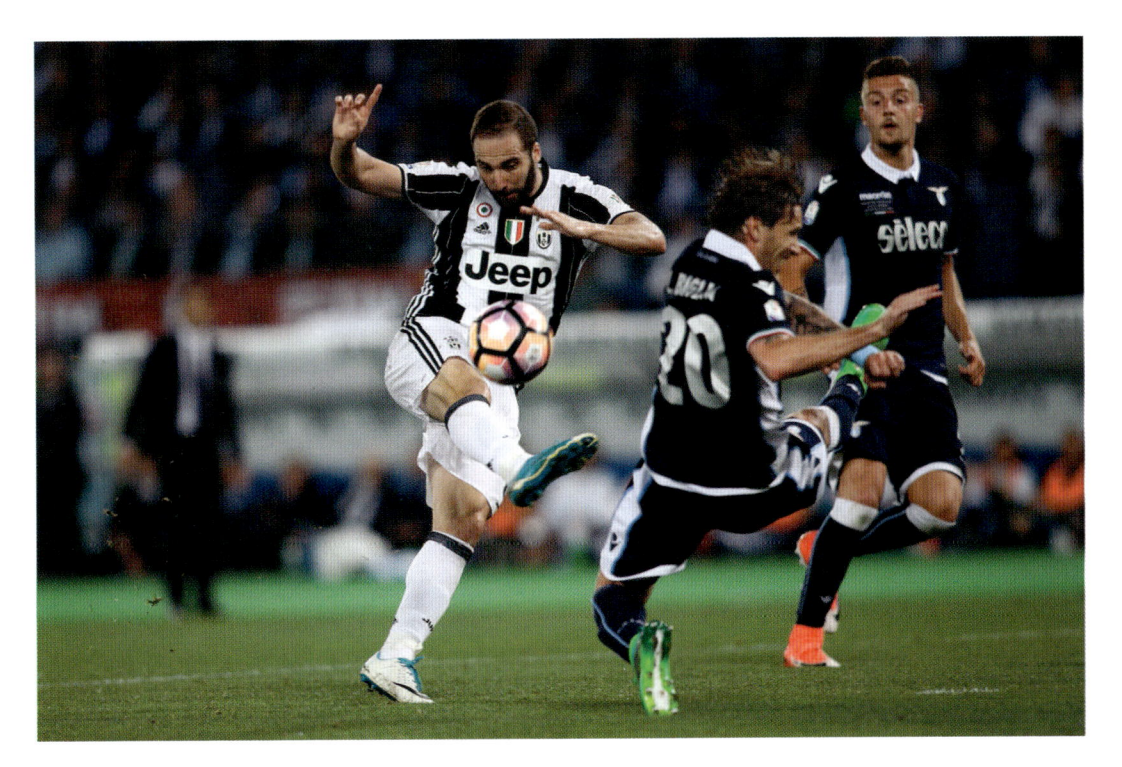

ABOVE: *A soccer match between S.S. Lazio vs. Juventus at the Stadio Olimpico in Rome, 2017.*

Sport

Italians love sports, both as spectators and participants. Association football, known as "football" in much of the world and as "soccer" in the United States, is the most popular sport in Italy. In Italy, football is a religion, each stadium is a Mount Olympus, and every player is a god. Italy has won the World Cup, the world championship, three times.

Luxury Goods

Italy has developed a cultural reputation as a world leader in fine clothing and luxury cars. Italian designers such as Gucci, Fendi, Prada, Salvatore Ferragamo, and Dolce and Gabanna lead the world in producing the **opulent** clothing and accessories worn by the rich and famous. Italian manufacturers

CITIZENS OF ITALY: PEOPLE, CUSTOMS & CULTURE

such as Maserati and Ferrari dominate the luxury car field, each producing luxury cars with features once thought possible only in science fiction.

Food

When it comes to food, Italy's reputation for **gastronomic** delights is world famous. Italian contributions to the world of cuisine include pizza and pastas such as spaghetti and linguini. Italian breads and soups are known for their heartiness. Wine and cheese are other popular Italian exports. The country is also home to a wide selection of sausages. Two of the most famous are bologna, a seasoned sausage of mixed meats originating in the Italian city that shares its name, and salami, another seasoned sausage.

ABOVE: The pizza is originally from Naples. It is traditionally cooked in a wood-fired oven.

EUROPEAN COUNTRIES TODAY: ITALY

Italian Pasta Bolognese

Ingredients
2 tablespoons butter
¼ pound of bacon, cut crosswise into ¼ inch strips
1 onion, chopped
½ pound ground beef
1 cup low-sodium chicken broth
½ cup dry white wine
2 tablespoons tomato paste
½ teaspoon dried oregano
¾ teaspoon salt
¼ teaspoon freshly ground black pepper
½ cup heavy cream
¾ pound spaghetti
basil to garnish

Directions
In a large frying pan, heat the butter and bacon over moderately low heat. Fry for 3 minutes, or until the bacon has rendered much of its fat. Add the onion and sauté, stiring occasionally, until it begins to soften, about 3 minutes longer. Stir in the ground beef and cook until the meat is no longer pink. Add broth, wine, tomato paste, oregano, salt and pepper. Simmer uncovered, stirring occasionally, until the sauce thickens, about 25 minutes. Stir in the cream and remove from the heat.

In a large pot of boiling, salted water, cook the spaghetti until done, about 12 minutes. Drain and toss in the sauce. Garnish with fresh basil.

Patate e Cipolle
(Potatoes With Onion)

Ingredients
2 pounds potatoes
2 pounds red onions
extra virgin olive oil
1 teaspoon fennel seeds
fresh rosemary
salt

Directions
Preheat the oven to 350 degrees F. Wash and peell onions and potatoes. Cut each into ½-inch slices. In an ovenproof dish, alternate layers of potatoes and onions, season with the oil, fennel, and salt. Bake in preheated oven for 30 minutes, or until the potatoes are crispy and golden. Serve warm. Garnish with rosemary.

CITIZENS OF ITALY: PEOPLE, CUSTOMS & CULTURE

Religion

Because most of the Italian population is Roman Catholic, many of the holidays and festivals that are a major part of Italian culture are based in Catholicism. Holidays and festivals, such as Christmas, Epiphany, and St. Stephen's Day, are all celebrated in accordance with Roman Catholic tradition.

ABOVE: *A traditional Easter parade, "La processione delle Vare" in Caltanissetta, Sicily.*

EUROPEAN COUNTRIES TODAY: ITALY

ABOVE: *The town of Corleone, Palermo, Sicily. The town has long been associated with the Mafia. Several Mafia bosses have come from there, including Tommy Gagliano, Jack Dragna, Giuseppe Morello, Michele Navarra, Luciano Leggio, Leoluca Bagarella, Salvatore Riina, and Bernardo Provenzano. Fictional characters in Mario Puzo's novel,* The Godfather, *are also associated with Corleone.*

The Mafia

One of Italy's most notorious cultural exports is the Mafia. The Mafia began in the Middle Ages in Sicily as a means of organizing and empowering the native population in resistance against their Norman and Arab conquerors. Etymologically, it is widely believed that the word *mafia* is derived from the Arabic word *mu'afa*, which generally is translated as "protected." The society was created to provide security for native Sicilians, but as the Mafia grew and time progressed, its focus moved from protection and strength to prostitution and murder. Italian immigrants brought the Mafia to the United States, and expulsion of Mafia members from Italy by the Italian government resulted in

🇮🇹 **CITIZENS OF ITALY: PEOPLE, CUSTOMS & CULTURE**

ABOVE: The old town of Bari is the capital of Apulia. The Mafia-type organization Sacra Corona Unita comes from this region.

more Mafia members entering the United States. Maintaining strong ties to their native land, they continued their organized crime life in their new homeland. The Mafia developed intricate levels of leadership that served to protect those at the top from prosecution in the event that a lower-level member was arrested. The Mafia has been portrayed in film and on television and as a result has developed an almost glamorous appeal. In Italy, there are several lesser-known units of organized crime that engage in the same drug trafficking, money laundering, and prostitution as the Mafia, such as the Camorra in the region of Italy known as Campania (where Naples is located) and the Sacra Corona Unita, or "United Sacred Crown," in southern Italy's Apulia region.

As famous as the Mafia is, it would be a mistake to equate Italy with crime. Other nations have their own version of organized crime—and Italy contributes far more than the Mafia to the international stage. Italy's food, art, and style all enrich the entire world.

Text-Dependent Questions

1. What is Griko?

2. When did the Renaissance start?

3. Who painted the *Mona Lisa*?

Research Project

Write a report on the history of organized crime in Italy.

Words to Understand

artifacts: Usually simple objects (such tools or ornaments) showing human workmanship or modification.

enclave: A distinct territorial, cultural, or social unit enclosed within a foreign territory.

infrastructure: The basic equipment and structures that are needed for a country to function properly.

BELOW: Rome is the capital city of Italy. It is a large, cosmopolitan city steeped in history. For 3,000 years, Rome has influenced the world's art, architecture, and culture. Ancient ruins such as the Forum and the Colosseum are legacies of the former Roman Empire. Within Rome, the enclave state of the Vatican City (headquarters of the Roman Catholic Church), has important works of art and architecture on display. St. Peter's Basilica, in the Vatican, is a popular tourist destination.

Chapter Five
THE FAMOUS CITIES OF ITALY

Italy is for the most part a rural nation, with its towns and villages nestled among rolling hills and mountainous landscapes. There are, however, many urban hubs where the majority of italy's industrial development and demographical diversity can be found. Cities such as Rome, Milan, Naples, and Turin are growing yearly in **infrastructure** and development.

Rome

The capital of Italy, and its largest city, is Rome. An ancient city dating back thousands of years, Rome is full of history, landmarks, and tourist attractions. Many areas of the city date back to Roman times and are preserved to this day. With 2.8 million inhabitants, the city of Rome can be quite cramped in some places. Italian cities are known for their small, narrow streets, and for the most part Rome is no exception. The historical sites range from ancient tombs, the Forum, and the Colosseum to medieval buildings. The seat of the Roman Catholic Church is in Vatican City, which is an **enclave** within the city of Rome. St. Peter's Basilica in the Vatican is a popular tourist destination.

ABOVE: The Colosseum in Rome is also known as the Flavian Amphitheater. It was built in 80 CE.

THE FAMOUS CITIES OF ITALY

Educational Video

A vacation travel guide to Italy's capital city Rome.

ABOVE: *The Trevi Fountain is the largest baroque fountain in Rome and is reputed to be the most beautiful in the world. A traditional legend holds that if visitors throw a coin into the fountain, they are ensured a return to Rome.*

EUROPEAN COUNTRIES TODAY: ITALY

ABOVE: Dating from 1721, the Spanish Steps link the Piazza di Spagna at the base with the Piazza Trinità dei Monti at the top. At the very top is the Trinità dei Monti Church.

Rome is quite accessible, with several airports bringing tourists to the city. Leonardo da Vinci International Airport, Giovanni Battista Pastine International Airport, and Aeroporto dell'Urbe can all be used to enter the city of Rome and the surrounding metropolitan districts.

THE FAMOUS CITIES OF ITALY

Vatican City

The state of the Vatican City is the seat of the Roman Catholic Church. It is an enclave in Rome, situated on the west bank of the Tiber River. It is the world's smallest fully independent state and has a population of just 1,000 people. Its medieval and Renaissance walls form its boundaries, except on the southeast at St. Peter's Square. Within the Vatican is St. Peter's Basilica, built during the fourth century and rebuilt during the sixteenth century. The Vatican is also home to other important cultural sites such as the Sistine Chapel and the Vatican Museums. The economy of the Vatican is supported by tourism.

EUROPEAN COUNTRIES TODAY: ITALY

Milan

Milan is Italy's second-largest city with 1.3 million people living within the city limits. Another historical city, Milan has several notable Roman monuments, such as the Columns of San Lorenzo and other ruins of its past glory. The city's main function in Italy's modern society and economy is as a financial center and a leader in the bustling fashion industry of Italy. The city, accessible to tourists through its Malpensa and Linate airports, is home to designers

ABOVE: *The Roman Columns of San Lorenzo are an important landmark and tourist attraction in Milan.*

73

THE FAMOUS CITIES OF ITALY

ABOVE: Situated on the Piazza del Duomo in Milan is the spectacularly beautiful Milan Cathedral.

Versace, Dolce and Gabbana, and Giorgio Armani. The Quadrilatero, the city's exclusive shopping area, is a stop for many tourists because of its unique mix of history and fashion.

Naples

Naples, with a population of 1 million people, is Italy's third-largest city. It is the traditional birthplace of pizza and home to the oldest opera house in Europe, the Teatro di San Carlo. The city also has one of Europe's oldest aquariums,

EUROPEAN COUNTRIES TODAY: ITALY

Mount Vesuvius

Mount Vesuvius is an active volcano located above the Bay of Naples and and is situated just nine miles from Naples. It is one of several volcanoes that form the Campanian volcanic arc and is the only volcano on mainland Europe to have erupted within the last hundred years.

Its most famous eruption was in 79 CE and led to the burying of several Roman settlements, including Pompeii and Herculaneum. The eruption ejected a cloud of stones, ash, and volcanic gases to a height of 21 miles (33 km) and spewed molten rock and pulverized pumice. Thousands died in the eruption, but exact numbers are unknown. The only surviving eyewitness account of the event consists of two letters by 18- year-old Pliny the Younger to the historian Tacitus. The last eruption of Mount Vesuvius occurred in 1944, during the height of the World War II, destroying US bomber planes stationed a few miles away.

THE FAMOUS CITIES OF ITALY

which can be found in La Villa Comunale, an area that was formerly a royal park. Museo Archeologico Nazionale Napoli, the National Archeological Museum of Naples, has a large collection of Roman **artifacts**, such as the Farnese Marbles, classical marble statues made by Roman sculptors of the

ABOVE: *The ancient center of Naples consists of small winding streets, many of which are now pedestrianized.*

EUROPEAN COUNTRIES TODAY: ITALY

ABOVE: Castel dell'Ovo (Italian for the "Egg Fortress") is located on a peninsula in the Bay of Naples.

Roman emperors, and figures in nature. It also houses replicas of ancient Greek statues that have been lost or destroyed. Naples, home to extensive catacombs, also has the Museo Nazionale de Capodimonte, which contains many works by Michelangelo and Raphael.

THE FAMOUS CITIES OF ITALY

Turin

The city of Turin has 921,485 residents, and with the three rivers (the Po, Dora Riparia, and Stura di Lanzo) running through the city, and the major industries (such as the Fiat car manufacturer's main factory within city limits), Turin is the most important city in northwest Italy. The host city for the 2006 Winter Olympics, it is Italy's fourth-largest city and, much like the rest of Italy, is rich in history. The Turin Shroud is housed in the cathedral of St. John the Baptist, and the Museo Egizio holds the second-largest collection of ancient Egyptian artifacts in the world. Home to many royal palaces and historical buildings that were named World Heritage Sites in 1997, the city of Turin's close proximity to the Italian Alps brings another group of yearly visitors to the area. The famous Italian football club, Juventus, calls the city of Turin its home, and many football enthusiasts from across the globe enjoy watching the world-class football that Juventus has to offer.

ABOVE: *A view of Turin city center. The Mole Antonelliana tower is in the foreground and the Alps are in the background.*

EUROPEAN COUNTRIES TODAY: ITALY

ABOVE: *Piazza San Carlo is one of the main city squares in Turin. It was laid out in the sixteenth and seventeenth centuries. Its buildings are examples of the baroque style.*

Text Dependent Questions

1. Where is the Colosseum?

2. Where is the center of the fashion industry?

3. What is Italy's third-largest city?

Research Project

Make a map of Italy and mark the major cities on it, making sure you include Rome, Venice, Naples, Turin, Florence, Milan, and Bologna.

Words to Understand

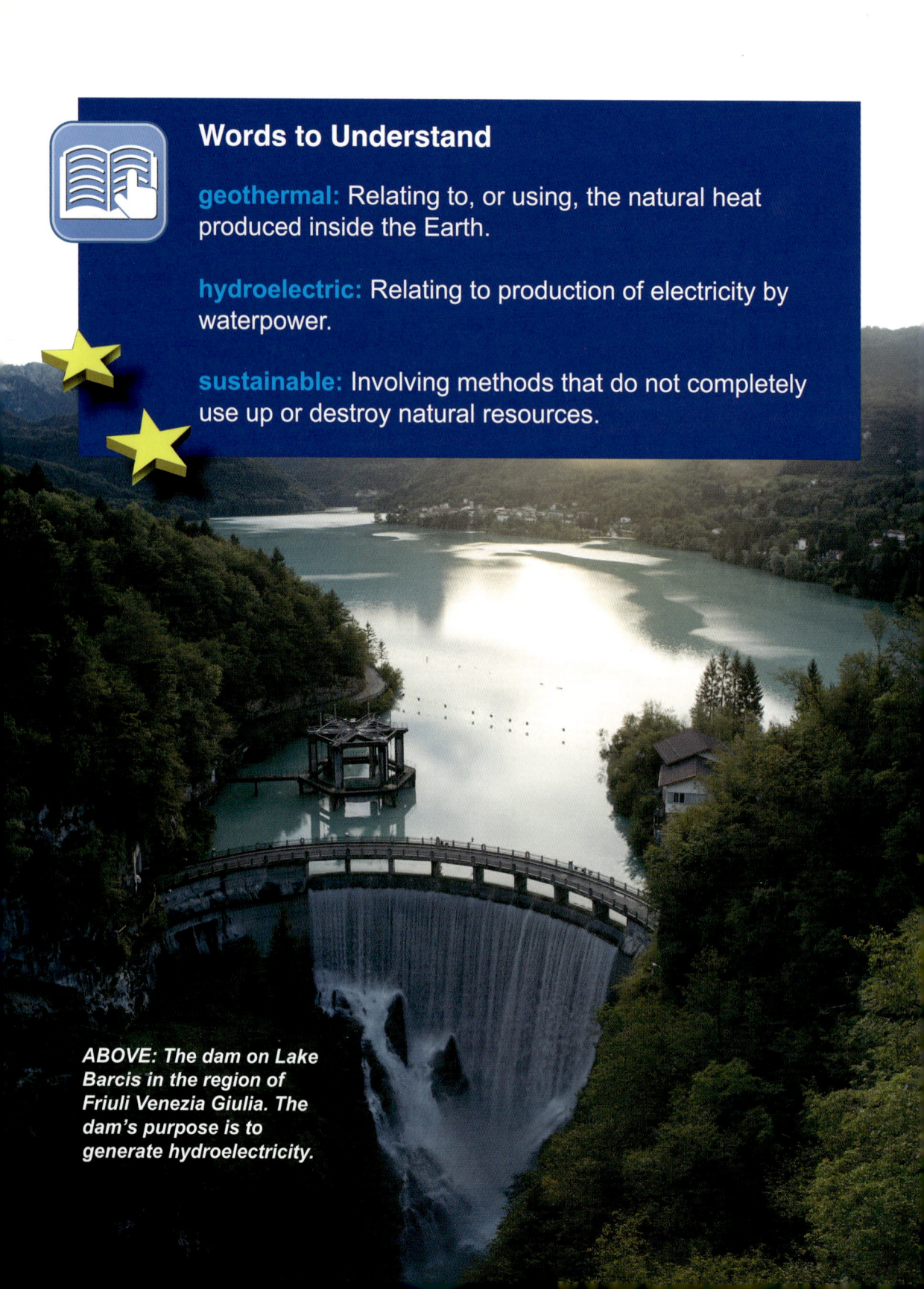

geothermal: Relating to, or using, the natural heat produced inside the Earth.

hydroelectric: Relating to production of electricity by waterpower.

sustainable: Involving methods that do not completely use up or destroy natural resources.

ABOVE: The dam on Lake Barcis in the region of Friuli Venezia Giulia. The dam's purpose is to generate hydroelectricity.

Chapter Six
A BRIGHT FUTURE FOR ITALY

Italy's future is uncertain. The solution to almost all its problems—women's rights, politics, the economy—all rely on whether Italians can begin to work together toward common goals.

Ultimately, however, one of the biggest issues facing the entire world has to do with global climate change. The economy of every nation in the world depends on the health of our planet in order to thrive. If the nations of the world fail to make caring for the Earth a priority, we will all suffer. Since Italians have often cared more about their own families and villages than they do the world at large, environmentalists are watching Italy to see how it will respond to the crisis of worldwide climate change. Will Italians take action to protect the environment and invest in **sustainable** forms of energy? Or will they stick their heads in the sand and insist on keeping things just as they have always been?

Many Italian communities are in fact making big changes to the way they get their energy. More than eight hundred cities and villages in Italy have built renewable-energy

ABOVE: Italian and EU flags.

A BRIGHT FUTURE FOR ITALY

ABOVE: The Milazzo Oil refinery in Sicily. Italy still relies greatly on carbon-based energy.

plants that make more energy than they use. This means that the communities actually earn money every year by selling their surplus energy. They then invest the funds back into their own communities. So in this case, Italians' tendency to focus on the smaller community versus the nation is actually helping the environment.

In recent years, Italy has led the way, overtaking other EU nations, in creating a consistent energy policy. Italy has many renewable energy sources available to it, including **geothermal**, solar, wind, and **hydroelectric**. Italy's renewable energy use has nearly tripled in less than a decade, from 5.6 percent in 2004 to 16.7 percent in 2013 and is on track to meet its 2020 target of 17.0 percent.

While Italy's government may consider the possibility of building more nuclear power plants, the 2011 Fukushima nuclear disaster in Japan has

EUROPEAN COUNTRIES TODAY: ITALY

ABOVE: A geothermal power plant in Larderello, Tuscany. Geothermal power plants use steam produced from reservoirs of hot water found a few miles or more below the Earth's surface to produce electricity. The steam rotates a turbine that activates a generator, which produces electricity.

A BRIGHT FUTURE FOR ITALY

ABOVE: *Italy has made great strides in developing renewable energy. These wind turbines are in the the Nebrodi Mountains, Sicily.*

EUROPEAN COUNTRIES TODAY: ITALY

worried Italians. For this reason, the government has decided to put all plans on hold before pursuing a nuclear strategy. Concerned Italians, especially young people, have voted overwhelmingly against a return to nuclear power, repealing regulation that allowed for the construction of new reactors in a national referendum. Despite being a pioneer of nuclear science and engineering, Italy is now unique in the world for having rejected this technology and also for actually closing its nuclear plants in line with this policy. Whenever there is

ABOVE: *In most Italian cities the car is still king, with relatively few people using bicycles. Cities such as Rome, shown above, can become both polluted and congested at times.*

A BRIGHT FUTURE FOR ITALY

controversy about nuclear energy, some Italians are convinced that nuclear plants can never be absolutely safe.

Big businesses in Italy, however, are more in favor of nuclear power, which they feel could benefit them through the availability of cheap energy, so there are always two sides of every argument. Meanwhile, other experts insist that renewable energy plants would achieve the same goal while at the same time stimulating Italy's scientific research and development community, which lags behind some other countries in the world—though is currently catching up.

ABOVE: Italy is an important exporter of foods to the rest of the world. Canning plants, such as this one in Parma, are dependent on competitive energy prices.

EUROPEAN COUNTRIES TODAY: ITALY

ABOVE: *Italy is in an enviable position when it comes to the fashion industry. Italian fashion houses dominate a great percentage of high-end fashion sales worldwide.*

A BRIGHT FUTURE FOR ITALY

ABOVE: *The Italian government, like many other governments in the world, needs to weigh up the pros and cons of developing more nuclear energy plants.*

Nuclear Energy Pros and Cons

People who are in favor of building nuclear plants point to the fact that the world's oil, coal, and gas supplies are running out. What's more, only a few countries have these resources, which means that countries that don't have their own oil or gas must depend on importing them from the countries that do. Nuclear plants provide jobs, promote research and development, and stimulate the economy.

People who are against building nuclear plants say that these plants are expensive to build; they require uranium, a very rare and expensive chemical element, which means that most countries will still need to depend on imports from other countries in order to get the necessary resources; and, most

EUROPEAN COUNTRIES TODAY: ITALY

important, nuclear plants produce radioactive waste. When something goes wrong—as it did at Chernobyl and Fukushima—these plants release dangerous radiation into the environment. Even if nothing ever goes wrong, the radioactive waste must be collected and then permanently contained in a safe way that does not endanger the environment, a problem that has not yet been totally solved.

Some experts wonder if this might be the Italians' opportunity to join together in a new way, to speak out with a unified voice to both their government and the entire world on one of the most important issues that faces the future of the entire world: sustainable energy.

If Italians start working together, who knows what they might accomplish?

Text Dependent Questions

1. Why is there opposition to nuclear energy?

2. What percentage of Italy's energy comes from renewables?

3. What happened at Fukushima in 2011?

Research Project

Write a report explaining why climate change is such a big issue for the future in Italy.

CHRONOLOGY

753 BCE	According to legend, twins Romulus and Remus found Rome.
509	The Roman Republic begins.
334–264	Rome begins to spread its colonial influence to the rest of the Italian Peninsula; Rome begins to mint coins.
49	Julius Caesar becomes the head of the Roman Republic.
27	Augustus Caesar the emperor of Rome.
43 CE	Romans occupy Britannia (Britain).
79	Mount Vesuvius erupts, burying the ancient city of Pompeii in ash.
313	Roman emperor Constantine declares Christianity the official religion of the empire and ends persecution of Christians.
476	Rome falls.
773–74	Charlemagne conquers Italy.
1252	First gold coins minted in Europe are made in Florence.
1348–49	The Black Death ravages Italy.
1452	Leonardo da Vinci is born in Anchiano, Italy.
1508–12	Michelangelo paints the ceiling of the Sistine Chapel.
1633	Astronomer and scientist Galileo is condemned in Rome.
1861	The Kingdom of Italy is founded with King Emmanuel II of Sardinia.
1915	Italy enters World War I on the side of the Allies.
1922	Mussolini is named prime minister of Italy; fascist rule begins.
1940	Italy enters World War II on the side of the Axis Powers.
1946	The monarchy is abolished, and the Republic of Italy is formed.
1949	Italy joins NATO.
1978	Former prime minister Aldo Moro kidnapped and murdered by left-wing armed group, the Red Brigades. Abortion legalised.
1992	The European Union begins, with Italy as one of its founding members.
1916	Paolo Gentiloni takes control of Italian politics.
2016	August earthquake rocks mountainous Appenine area of central Italy, causing extensive damage and casualties. Nearly 300 people are killed, most of them in the town of Amatrice.

FURTHER READING & INTERNET RESOURCES

Further Reading

Belford, Ros. Boulton, Susie. Catling, Christopher. Cole, Sam. Duncan, Paul. Ercoli, Olivia. Gumbel, Andrew. Jepson, Tim. McDonald, Ferdie. Shaw, Jane. *DK Eyewitness Travel Guide: Italy*. London: DK, 2018.

Clark, Gregor. Bonetto, Cristian. Christiani, Kerry. Di Duca, Marc. Dragicevich, Peter. Garwood, Duncan. Hardy, Paula. Maxwell, Virginia. Raub, Kevin. *Lonely Planet Italy (Travel Guide)*. London: Lonely Planet Publications, 2018.

Mason, David S. *A Concise History of Modern Europe: Liberty, Equality, Solidarity.* London: Rowman & Littlefield, 2015.

McCormick, John. *Understanding the European Union: A Concise Introduction*. London: Palgrave Macmillan, 2017.

Internet Resources

Lonely Planet: Italy
https://www.lonelyplanet.com/italy

Italian Tourism Official Website
http://www.italia.it/en/home.html

Italy: CIA World Factbook
https://www.cia.gov/library/publications/the-world-factbook/geos/it.html

The Official Website of the European Union
europa.eu/index_en.htm

Publisher's note:
The websites listed on this page were active at the time of publication. The publisher is not responsible for websites that have changed their addresses or discontinued operation since the date of publication. The publisher will review and update the website list upon each reprint.

INDEX

A
Abortion rights, 38
Adriatic Sea, 11, 13
Aeroporto dell'Urbe, 71
Agnosticism, 9
Agriculture, 44, 49
Albania, 33
Albanians, 56
Alfa Romeo, 45
Allies, 32
    invasion, 33
Alps, 8, 11, 13, 78
Alsace-Lorraine, 33
Antony, Marc, 26
Apennine Mountains, 8, 11, 13, 17, 19
Apulia, 66, 67
Arabs, 30, 56, 65
Armani, 52
Army, 33
Art nouveau style, 34, 58–59
Art of War, The (Machiavelli), 59
Asti, 42
Atheism, 9
Augustus, 26
    Romulus, 27
Austria, 7, 11, 30, 31, 46
Automotive industry, 45, 62
Avalanches, 14–16

B
Bagarella, Leoluca, 65
Balbo, Italo, 32
Ballarò market, 51
Banking crisis, 39
Bari, 66
Baroque period, 59
Bay of Naples, 75, 77
Belgium, 41, 49
Bianchi, Michele, 32
Bilingualism, 55
Birth rate, 9
Blackshirts, 32
Blitzkrieg, 33
Bono, Emilio De, 32
Borders, 7

Britannia, 26
Bronze Age, 23
Brussels, 40
Byzantine Empire, 27, 30

C
Caesar, Julius, 26, 27
    murder, 26, 27
Cagliari, 13
Caltanissetta, 64
Camera dei Deputati. *See* Chamber of Deputies (Camera dei Deputati)
Camorra, 67
Campania, 15, 67
Campanian volcanic arc, 75
Campo dei Miracoli (Field of Miracles), 28
Camuccini, Vincenzo, 27
Capital, 68, 69
Caracalla, 46
Carbonari, 31
Carrara, 43
    marble, 43
Carthage, 25
Castel dell'Ovo (Egg Fortress), 77
Castelluccio di Norcia, 19
Chamberlin, Neville, 33
Chamber of Deputies (Camera dei Deputati), 34, 35
Chamois, 17
Charlemagne, 30
Charles VIII, 30
Chernobyl disaster, 89
Chianti, 50
    wine, 50
China, 49
Christianity, 9
Christmas, 64
Cities, 69–79
City-states, 30
Civil War, 36
Classical period, 59
Climate, 7, 13–14
    change, 81
Cloning, 18
Colombo, Cristoforo. *See*

Columbus, Christopher
Colosseum, 68, 69
Columbus, Christopher, 30
Como lake, 13
Constitution, 31, 33
Constitutional charter, 36
Constitutional Court (Corte Costituzionale), 35
Corleone, 65
Corsica, 13, 18
Corte Costituzionale. *See* Constitutional Court (Corte Costituzionale)
Council of Ministers, 35
Craxi, Bettino, 33
Crime, 31
Cristoforo, Bartolomeo, 59
Currency, 41, 49
Cyprus, 18

D
Dark Ages, 58
"Death of Julius Caesar, The" (Camuccini), 27
Death rate, 9
Democrats, 35, 38
Dining, 8
Disasters, natural, 14–16
Dolce and Gabanna, 61, 74
Dolomites mountains, 12
Dora Riparia river, 78
Dragna. Jack, 65

E
Earthquakes, 16
Easter, 57, 64
Economy, 39, 43–53, 81
    global recession, 46, 48, 49, 50, 51, 53
    inflation, 27
    postwar, 33
Egg Fortress. *See* Castel dell'Ovo (Egg Fortress)
Electoral college, 35
Elevation, 7
Emilia-Romagna, 43
Emmanuel II, 31
Employment, 44

INDEX

Energy, 45
   geothermal, 82, 83
   hydroelectricity, 80, 82
   nuclear, 82–83, 85–86, 88–88
   renewable, 81–82, 84
   solar, 82
   sustainable, 81, 89
   wind, 82, 84
England, 31, 33
Environment, 38
Epiphany, 64
Ethiopia, 33
   declaration of war on, 31
Ethnic groups, 9, 38
Etruscans, 23–24, 25
Euro, 41, 49
European
   Coal and Steel Community, 41
   Community, 41
   Council, 40
   debt crisis, 39
   Economic Community, 41
   mouflon, 18
European Union (EU), 35–36, 38
   autonomy, 40
   flag, 81
   formation, 40–41
   issues in, 35–36, 38
   laws, 40
   members, 40, 41
   Parliament Building, 40
   single market, 41
   values, 40
Executive branch, 35
Exports, 45, 49, 86

F
Families, 55
Farnese Marbles, 76
Fascism, 87
   rise of, 32–33
Fashion, 61–62, 73, 74
Fendi, 61
Ferdinand I, 30
Ferragamo, Salvatore, 61
Ferrari, 43, 45, 62
Fertility rate, 9
Fiat, 45
Field of Miracles. *See* Campo dei Miracoli (Field of Miracles)
Flag, 8, 81
Flavian Amphitheater. *See* Colosseum
Florence, 30, 45, 54, 58, 59
Food, 62–63, 86
Football, 61, 78
France, 7, 11, 30, 31, 40, 41, 45, 46, 49
Franco, Francisco, 33
Franks, 30
Frescoes, 59
Friuli Venezia Giulia, 80
Fukushima disaster, 82–83, 89
Funes Valley, 12

G
Gagliano, Tommy, 65
Galleria Vittorio Emanuele II shopping mall, 52
Garda lake, 13
Garibaldi, Giuseppe, 31–32
Gas and oil, 45
Gauls, 25
Gentiloni, Paolo, 35, 36, 37, 38
Geography, 7
Germany, 45, 49
Giorgio Armani, 74
Giovanni Battista Pastine International Airport, 71
Godfather, The (Puzo), 65
Government, 23–42
Great Plain. *See* Piano Grand (Great Plain)
Greece, 48, 55
Gross domestic product (GDP), 44, 49
Gucci, 52, 61

H
Habsburg Dynasty, 30
Hazards, 7
Herculaneum, 75
History, 23–42
Hitler, Adolf, 33
Holy
   Roman Empire, 30
   See. *See* Vatican City

I
Iberian Peninsula, 26
Ides of March, 27
Immigration, 39, 56, 58, 65
Imports, 45, 49
Independence, 30, 31
Indo-European-speaking tribes, 23
Industries, 44, 45, 49
Infant mortality rate, 9
Infrastructure, 69
Intragovernmentalism, 36
Invasion, French, 30
Ionian Sea, 11
Islam, 9, 56, 58
Islands, 13
Italian
   language, 9, 56
   Pasta Bolognese, 63
   Popular Party, 35
   Renewal Party, 35
Italians, 9

J
Japan, 82–83
Jehovah's Witnesses, 9
Judaism, 58
Judiciary, 35
Juventus, 78

K
Kingdom of Italy, 31
Kurds, 58

L
Lake Barcis, 80
Lakes, 13
Languages, 9
Lardarello, 83
Last Supper, The (Vinci), 59
Latin
   League, 24–26
   War, 24–26

93

INDEX

Latium, 24
Leggio, Luciano, 65
Lent, 57
Leonardo da Vinci International Airport, 71
Leonardo da Vinci (Vinci), 58
Lepidus, Marcus, 26
Libya, 32, 39
Life expectancy, 9
Ligurian Sea, 11
Linate airport, 73
Literacy rate, 9
Location, 7
Lombards, 30
Louvre, 26
Luxembourg, 41

M

Maastricht Treaty, 41
Machiavelli, Niccolò, 58, 59
Mafia, 65–67
Maggiore lake, 13
Magna Grecia, 56
Malpensa airport, 73
Map, 6
Maranello, 43
March on Rome, 32
Marriage, 55
　same-sex, 38
Marshall Plan, 33
Maserati, 45, 62
Mattarella, Sergio, 35
Medieval period, 30
Mediterranean Sea, 7, 11, 13
Merger Treaty, 41
Mesolithic period, 23
Michaelangelo, 43, 59, 77
Middle Ages, 65
Migration rates, 9
Milan, 30, 46, 48, 52, 60, 69, 73–74
　Cathedral, 74
　Central railroad station, 46
Milazzo Oil refinery, 82
Mole Antonelliana tower, 78
Mona Lisa (Vinci), 59
Money, 38
Mont Blans. *See* Monte Bianco de Courmayer
Monte Bianco de Courmayer, 7, 11
Morello, Giuseppe, 65
Moscato d'Asti, 42
Mount
　Etna, 14
　Vesuvius, 14, 15, 75
Mountains, 7, 8, 11, 12, 13, 16, 19
Mudslides, 14–16
Museo
　Archeologico Nazionale Napoli (National Archaeological Museum of Naples), 76
　Egizio, 78
　Nationale de Capodimonte, 77
Music, 59–60
　current, 59
　notation, 59
Mussolini, Benito, 32, 33
　execution, 33
　expulsion, 33

N

Naples, 62, 67, 69, 74–77
National Archaeological Museum of Naples. *See* Museo, Archeologico Nazionale Napoli (National Archaeological Museum of Naples)
Navarra, Michele, 65
Nebrodi Mountains, 84
Neolithic period, 23
Neptune, 23
Netherlands, 41, 49
New World, 30
Niccolò, Machiavelli (Tito), 58
Norcia, 16
Normans, 30, 56, 65
North Africa, 56

O

Octavius, 26
Old Bridge. *See* Ponte Vecchio (Old Bridge)
Olive tree, 18
Olympics, 78
Opera, 59

P

Palazzo
　del Quirinale, 36, 38
　Madama, 36
　Montecitorio, 34, 36
Paleolithic period, 23
Palermo, 51, 65
Paris, 26
Parlamento. *See* Parliament (parlamento)
Parliament (parlamento), 35, 36
Parma, 50, 86
Parmesan cheese, 50
Pasta, 62
Patate e Cipolle, 63
People, 9, 55–67
Phillip I, 30
Phoenicians, 56
Piano Grand (Great Plain), 19
Piazza
　del Duomo, 74
　di Spagna, 71
　San Carlo, 79
　Trinità dei Monti, 71
Piedmont, 42
Piombo, Sebastiano del, 30
Pizza, 62
Plants, 18, 21
Pliny the Younger, 75
Political parties, 35
Pollution, 16, 85
Pompeii, 15, 75
Ponte Vecchio (Old Bridge), 54
Population, 9
　age, 9
　growth rate, 9
Po river, 13, 78
Portofino, 11
Potatoes with Onion, 63
Prada, 52, 61
President, 35, 36
Prime minister, 35, 36, 37, 38
Prince, The (Machiavelli), 59
Processione delle Vare, 64

INDEX

Protestantism, 9, 58
Provenzano, Bernardo, 65
Puccini, Giacomo, 59, 60
Punic War, 25
Puzo, Mario, 65
Pyrrhic War, 25

Q
Quadrilatero, 74

R
Railroad, 45–46
Raphael, 77
Recipes, 63
Redshirts, 31
Regionalism, 31, 39, 43
Religion, 9, 64
Remus, 24
Renaissance, 54, 58–59
Republic, 35
Riina, Salvatore, 65
Roman
 artifacts, 76
 Catholicism, 9, 58, 64, 72
 Columns of San Lorenzo, 73
 Empire, 22, 26–27
 Forum, 22, 68, 69
Romance language, 56
Rome, 13, 23, 34, 46, 56, 59, 61, 68, 69–74, 85
 birth of, 24
 fall of, 26–27
 growth, 24–26
 Senate, 26
Rome-Berlin Pact, 33
Romulus, 24

S
Sacra Corona Unita, 66, 67
Samnites, 25
Samnite Wars, 25
San Marino, 7, 11
Santa Maddalena, 12
Sardinia, 7, 13, 18, 31
Sausages, 62
Scala, La. *See* Teatro alla Scala (La Scala)

Senate (Senato della Repubblica), 35
Senato della Repubblica. *See* Senate (Senato della Repubblica)
Service sector, 44
Shrove Tuesday, 57
Sicilian language, 56
Sicily, 7, 13, 30, 46, 51, 55, 56, 63, 65, 82, 84
Sistine Chapel, 59, 72
Soccer, 61
Social
 activism, 31
 life, 55
Spain, 33, 45, 49
Spanish, 56
 Civil War, 33
 Steps, 71
Sports, 61
Spumante, 42
St.
 John the Baptist, 78
 Peter's Basilica, 68, 69, 72
 Peter's Square, 72
 Stephen's Day, 64
Stacchini, Ulisse, 46
Stadio Olimpico, 61
Standard of living, 39
Stura di Lanzo river, 78
Supranationalism, 36
Switzerland, 7, 11, 46, 49

T
Tacitus, 75
Teatro alla Scala (La Scala), 60
Terrain, 7
Tiber river, 13, 72
Tito, Santi di, 58
Tourism, 45, 47, 49, 72. *See* Colosseum
Tower of Pisa, 28–29
Treaties of Rome, 41
Treaty of Paris, 41
Trevi Fountain, 23, 70
Trinità dei Monti Church, 71
Truffles, 20
Tunisia, 25, 46

Turin, 69, 78–79
 Shroud, 78
Turkey, 58
 declaration of war on, 31
Tuscany, 10, 20, 83
Tyrrhenian Sea, 11

U
Umbria, 16, 19
UniCredit, 49
 building, 48
Unification, 31–32, 43
Union of Democrats for Europe, 35
United
 Kingdom, 49
 States, 33, 36, 45, 46, 48, 49, 67
University of Teramo, 18

V
Vatican
 City, 7, 11, 68, 69, 72
 Museums, 72
Vecchi, Cesare Maria De, 32
Venice, 30, 45, 47
 Carnival, 57
Verdi, Giuseppe, 59, 60
Versace, 74
Victor Emmanuel, 8
 III, 33
Villa Comunale, La, 76
Vinci, Leonardo da, 58, 59
Volcano, 14, 15, 75

W
War of the Spanish Succession, 30
West Germany, 40, 41
Wildlife, 16–18
Wine, 42, 50, 62
World Heritage sites, 45, 78
World War
 I, 32
 II, 33, 40, 75

Z
Zucchero, 59

95

Picture Credits

All images in this book are in the public domain or have been supplied under license by © Shutterstock.com. The publisher credits the following images as follows:

Page 8: Stansilav Samoylik, pages 11, 66: Anton_Ivanov, pages 16, 43: Dymtro Surkov, page 20: Knyazufoto, page 34: Shevchenko Andrey, page 37: Cristiano Barni, page 38: PriceM, page 40: Roman Yanushevsky, page 42: Daniela Pelazza, page 44: Paolo G, page 46: Pio3, page 47: Tupungato, page 50: Alexander Mazurkevich, page 51: Yulia Grigoryeva, page 52: Pcruciatti, page 60: Walencienne, page 61: Marco Laobucci EPP, page 64: Pecold, page 72: Georgios Tsichlis, page 75: Valipatov, page 76: Trabantos, page 84: Pxl.store, page 86: Alessia Pierdomincio, page 87: Tania Volobueva, page 88: Rostislav Glinsky.

To the best knowledge of the publisher, all images not specifically credited are in the public domain. If any image has been inadvertently uncredited, please notify the publisher, so that credit can be given in future printings.

Video Credits

Page 12 Geography Now!: http://x-qr.net/1H9H
page 24 Top5s: http://x-qr.net/1CtX
page 57 Datacube: http://x-qr.net/1H8g
page 70 Expedia: http://x-qr.net/1D3J

Author

Dominic J. Ainsley is a freelance writer on history, geography, and the arts and the author of many books on travel. His passion for traveling dates from when he visited Europe at the age of ten with his parents. Today, Dominic travels the world for work and pleasure, documenting his experiences and encounters as he goes. He lives in the south of England in the United Kingdom with his wife and two children.